AmericanGirl Library

party secrets

by Sarah Jane Brian
illustrated by Debra Dixon

Who to Invite, Must-Dance Music, Most-Loved Munchies & Foolproof Fun!

Published by Pleasant Company Publications

Questions or comments?
Call 1-800-845-0005, or write:
American Girl
P.O. Box 620497
Middleton, WI 53562-0497

Visit our Web site at **americangirl.com**

Printed in China

03 04 05 06 07 08 LEO 10 9 8 7 6 5 4 3 2 1

Editorial Development: Julie Williams
Art Direction: Camela Decaire, Chris David
Design: Camela Decaire
Production: Kendra Pulvermacher, Mindy Rappe, Jeannette Bailey
Photography: Jamie Young; marshmallow and ice cream sundae bar, page 34, Mike Walker; sandwich cookies, page 35, Mike Walker

All the instructions in this book have been tested. Results from testing were incorporated into this book. Nonetheless, all recommendations and suggestions are made without any guarantees on the part of Pleasant Company Publications. Because of differing tools, ingredients, conditions, and individual skills, the publisher disclaims liability for any injuries, losses, or other damages that may result from using the information in this book.

Cataloging-in-Publication Data available from the Library of Congress

Dear Party Girl,

We've been planning and throwing parties in the pages of ***American Girl*** **magazine** for more than ten years. Now we've collected our secrets to share with you. Whether you're planning your first party or your fifth, ***Party Secrets*** has all the inside information you'll need to host a fabulous bash for you and your friends, including

- invitation etiquette
- dreamy theme ideas
- decorating tips
- dance how-tos
- snack shortcuts
- quick 'n' easy crafts

and lots more!

You'll also learn how to steer clear of common party problems, and you'll get the scoop on being a gracious guest when you're invited to someone else's shindig. Plus, the **pull-out Party Checklists** will guarantee that your party goes as smoothly as icing on a cake!

So get ready... get set... celebrate!

Your friends at American Girl

Contents

Party Secret #1

Plan Ahead.

You're having a party, and you just can't wait for the **fun** to begin! But don't let the days slip by **just dreaming** about throwing the best bash ever. **Make it happen** by planning all the **delicious details.** The more things you think about, decide on, and do **ahead of time,** the more fun you'll have on party day.

Decisions,

First things first. When and where should your party happen? And what kind of party do you want to have? Pick the answers that fit you best.

When?

If you want to have a party . . .

a. when everyone who's invited isn't busy doing something else . . .

b. when you can do a certain activity like swimming or a sleepover . . .

Where?

If your home . . .

a. has lots of space . . .

b. is cozy but small . . .

What?

If you love . . .

a. coming up with lots of fun ideas as you plan every detail . . .

b. not having to spend too much time on the details, just as long as you have fun . . .

Decisions!

Then pick . . .

a. a day that doesn't fall on a long week-end or holiday, when some guests may be busy or out of town.

b. a day and time that's best for what you'll be doing. Fridays or Saturdays are best for sleepovers. And weekend afternoons are perfect for swimming and a barbecue. If you want to celebrate at a place like a public pool, call ahead to make sure that the location will be open on your party day, and make a reservation before you send out invitations.

Think about . . .

a. hosting a party at home, where everything you need is right at hand.

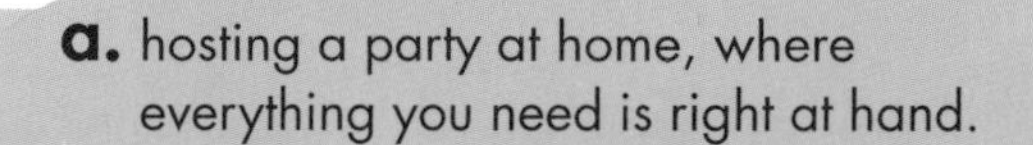

b. taking your party on the road. Many places, like movie theaters and theme restaurants, offer special party packages, so you can celebrate with plenty of space for you and your pals.

You may want to . . .

a. throw a party with interesting drinks, food, and games that all tie into a theme.

b. go theme-free and just entertain your guests with tried-and-true activities and favorite munchies.

What to Do at Your To-Do

How will you fill your party time? Circle the things that you want to do.

sleep over

lip-synch

munch a bunch

go see a flick

swim

giggle

Perfect Plan

Timing is everything! Once you decide what you'll be doing at your party, write out a schedule of activities like the one below, listing things in an order that makes sense. By allowing about 15 to 30 minutes for each activity, you'll get an idea of how long your party should be.

Noon–12:30
Snack and play games to help guests relax.

12:30–1:30
Dance, play sports, or get crafty. This will allow you and your guests to build up an appetite! If you're using glue or paint in your crafts, you'll want to finish early so that they'll have time to dry before the end of the party.

1:30–2:00
Eat! Chow down toward the end of the party, so that guests won't be too full to do all the activities you planned.

2:00–2:30
Dance or play more games.

2:30–3:00
Open presents and hand out favors.

Dream Themes

Ooh-La-La Spa

Break out the fuzzy slippers and pamper yourselves with face masks and manicures.

Come as Your Favorite Cartoon Character

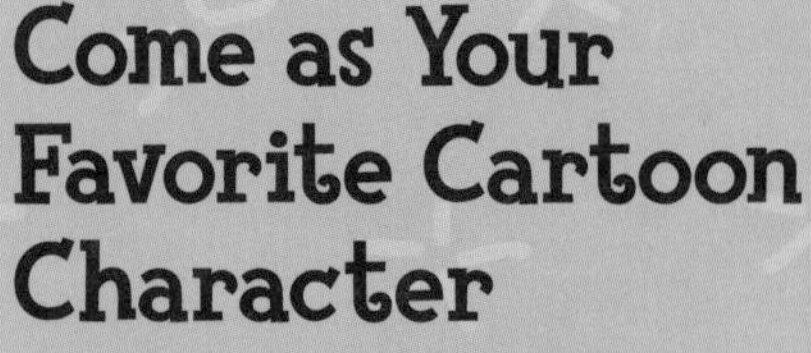

Imagine the fun with Bubbles, Spongebob, and Lisa Simpson all in the same room!

Poetry Slam

Set up your party space to look like a funky coffee-house, pass out berets, drink hot chocolate, and read poems aloud.

Paradise Island

Host a truly tropical to-do with flower lei necklaces, hula dancing, and fruity punch served with little umbrellas in the glasses.

All Skate

It's a party on wheels! Strap on the skates and roll around all day long.

Pick a Decade

. . . and play the part—50s sock hoppers, 60s hippies, 70s disco divas, or 80s big-hair material girls.

Celeb Celebration

Dress up like glamorous movie stars and videotape your own movie at the party. Give an award to each guest for her stunning performance!

Fiesta!

Have a south-of-the-border slumber party with a burrito bar, sombreros, and Spanish lingo, too . . . olé!

Game Show Gala

Set up versions of your favorite TV game shows around your house. You get to be the host! Come on down!

Backyard Survivor

Pitch a tent for a wild night outside with your guests. Don't forget the flashlights, tiki cups, and bandannas.

Dinner Party

Make an elegant sit-down dinner for your guests. Set the table with the good china (ask Mom first!) and fancy seating cards. Serve mock-tails before the first course. Formal attire required!

Crystal Ball

Have a family member dress up as a fortune teller, give the Magic 8-Ball a workout, make predictions, and pass out lucky charms as favors.

Dog Day

Celebrate your dog's birth-day! Play "Doggie in the Middle," serve bone-shaped cookies to your guests, and treat your pooch to a canine cake from a pet bakery.

Live & in Concert

. . . you and your friends! Set up a stage, dress like rock stars, lip-synch to music, play tam-bourines or air guitar, and do dance routines. It's a sold-out show!

Who's Invited?

Think About It

Deciding on the guest list may be the toughest part of planning your party. Make it easier by giving yourself some time to think about it. List the people you plan to invite several days before you send the invitations. That way, you'll have a chance to change your mind if you need to.

Check In

Go over the invite list with your parents. Is there a limit to the number of guests you can have? Is it O.K. to invite boys?

How to Pick & Choose

•Invite friends who you have the best time with or who will be the most fun.

•Think about inviting new friends or someone you would like to know better.

•Consider inviting a friend from camp or from across town who you don't see very often.

•Don't be tempted to invite only the more popular kids. You won't have a good time if you spend the whole party trying to impress people.

•Don't feel that you have to invite someone as a "payback" or because she invited you to her party.

•Make sure that no matter who you invite, you'll have fun!

Problem Pals?

You're great friends with two girls who would rather have their braces tightened than spend one hour in the same room together. Maybe one has even threatened to skip your party if the other girl is invited! **Don't be pressured** to choose between your pals. Instead, invite them both and ask them to declare a temporary truce—for your sake.

Things to think about . . .

At a Boy/Girl Party. . .

- You'll find out what boys act like when they're not in school.

- You can invite boys who are your friends.

- You'll have a chance to talk with your crush and get to know him better.

- Most boys travel in packs. If you invite one, he'll want to bring a friend or two . . . or three! Plan for a bigger party rather than a smaller one.

But at an All-Girl Party. . .

- You can talk about boys and other girl stuff!

- You can do things that boys wouldn't like to do, like try out new hairdos and paint toenails.

- You or your guests might be a little uncomfortable around boys. If you think this might happen, leave the boys out of it so you can be yourselves and have more fun!

Create a Buzz

Give your guests irresistible invites with all the juicy details.

Set the tone and **theme of the party** with art and words. Give the party a name!

Give the **start and end times** of your party so that your friends' parents will know when to pick them up. You can't party forever, you know!

Ask guests to **R.S.V.P.**–that's French for "call and let me know if you're coming or not!"

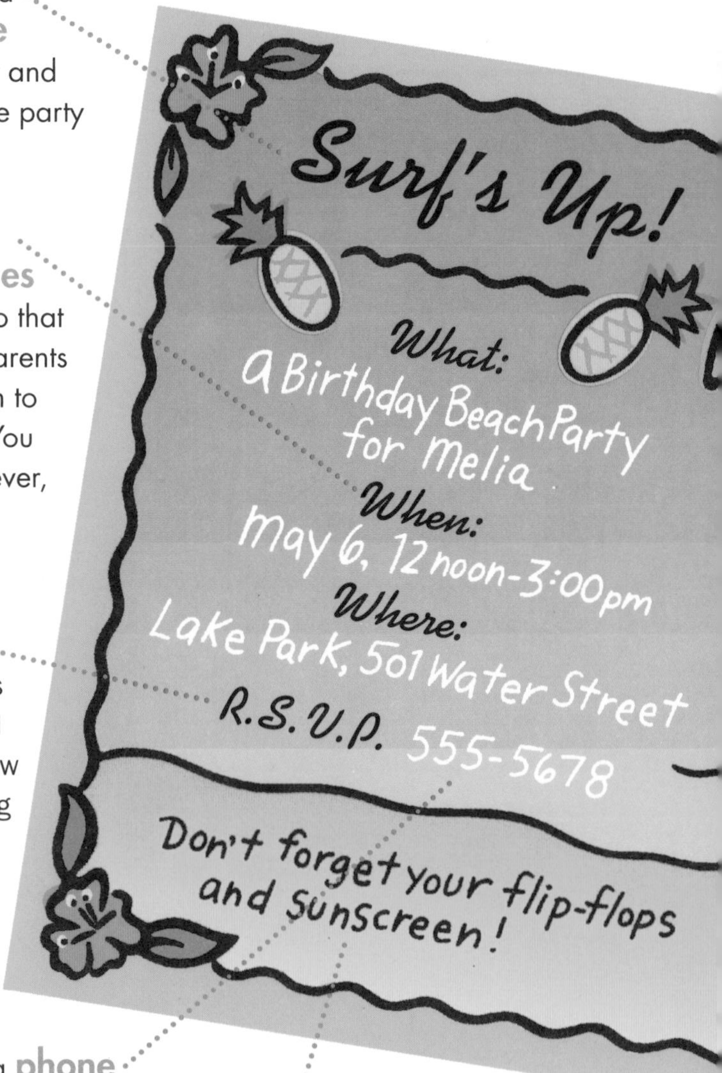

Provide a **phone number** or e-mail address for respond-ing and last-minute questions.

Add special instructions on what to bring or wear.

Include **directions** or a map to the party location. (You can put this on the invitation or on a separate sheet.)

Invitation Q&A

When should I give out my invitations?

Give your guests their invitations at least three weeks in advance so that they'll be less likely to have made other plans for that date.

What's the best way to get the invitations into guests' hands?

Mail or e-mail the invitations rather than handing them out at school. That way anyone not invited won't feel left out.

So how do I keep the party a "secret" from those not invited?

Avoid hurt feelings by letting invited guests know that you can invite only a certain number of friends. Ask them not to talk about the party around others who aren't invited.

What should I do if someone who's not invited asks to come?

Politely explain that you can have only a limited number of guests. Caving in would break your agreement with your parents about the size of your party. Also, you could end up with even more would-be guests clamoring for invitations.

Party Crew

Even the most fabulous hostess can't pull off a party all by herself. A few weeks before the big day, ask your parents or sibs to help with these party jobs.

Chef

Keeps the munchies coming, grills the burgers, or orders the pizza

Shopper

Helps you decide what and how much to buy

Decorator

Helps you blow up balloons, twist streamers, and arrange the party room

Photographer/ Videographer

Hangs around the fringes of the party scene, snapping photos or filming party doings

DJ

Helps plan what songs to play, keeps *your* favorites in heavy rotation, and takes requests from guests

Lighting Engineer

Transforms the living room into a dance floor with string lights and strobe lights

Coat Check

Takes guests' coats as people arrive

Kidding Around

Where will your kid brother and sister be during your party? If you want a strict no-siblings policy, perhaps they can go to a friend's house that day. If they will be around, try to include them in the party somehow. Maybe your sister could serve punch, or your brother could be in charge of hanging up coats. If your sibs are involved in the party, they may be less likely to disrupt it.

Party Animal

Does your pet like to mingle with strangers? If so, you may want to give her a good brushing so that she looks purr-fect for the party. If not, arrange to keep her separated from the crowd in a closed-off area, such as the basement. But if you think she'll howl, yowl, or bark the whole time, ask if she can stay with a friend or neighbor on your party day.

Here's how to pull it off.

1 To **avoid suspicion,** hold the party a few days before or after the person's birthday (or whatever event you're celebrating). Another trick: schedule the festivities for an unusual time of day, like the morning.

2 If you live with the guest of honor, **prepare** everything for the party—invitations, food, and decorations—at a friend's house. Have guests gather the goodies on party day and show up at your door all together. Surprise!

3 Would you rather **set up** the party ahead of time? Better have a good excuse to get the guest of honor out of the house. You'll need lots of time to get everything ready—a nice two-hour movie might just work. And ask guests to arrive 15 minutes before the girl of honor is due back.

4 Setting up the surprise at a different house can work well. Tell the girl of honor she's going to a party for someone else, and **she'll never suspect** a thing!

5 Most important, write "It's a Surprise Party!" on the invitations—in BIG letters. Better yet, **call the guests** before you send out the invites and give them the scoop on your surprise-party plans.

Did Someone Spill the Beans?

If the secret gets out, go ahead with your plans anyway—it's still a party!

Surprising Ideas

- Turn out the lights about **five minutes before** the girl of honor is due to arrive.

- Ask guests to stay away from windows and suggest that they duck behind a couch or hide around a corner before the girl of honor comes into the party room or house. Keep voices to a whisper.

- Have someone **watch for the girl of honor** and let everyone know when to get ready to jump and shout.

- Don't leave telltale signs of guests outside the house where they can be seen. **Hide scooters or bikes** in a garage or park cars down the street.

Party Smarts

Remember that it's *your* party.

Friends might give you lots of ideas about themes, people to invite, or what to serve—and they may be good ones, too! But don't feel pressured to accept them. You'll have a better time doing what *you* truly want to do.

Party Secret #2

Get Set!

Next to planning, prepping is the most important step in making sure your party goes off without a hitch. There are rooms to **decorate,** food to **make,** and maybe even a cake to **bake!** Use all your "just-can't-wait" anticipation to put the finishing touches on your party.

Party Palace

Make room for fun!

Remove Mom's antique vase or other breakable, treasured items from the room.

Hang a bead curtain in the doorway so that everyone can make a dramatic entrance to your party!

Scoot chairs and tables up along the wall to make plenty of space in the middle of the room. Clear an area large enough for a dance floor.

Put wastebaskets in spots where they're going to be needed, like next to the food or craft table.

String white or colored twinkle lights to create a party mood. Switch white lightbulbs to colored ones.

Gather up everything you'll need for games and activities, and keep it in one convenient spot. Stack party CDs next to the CD player, and you're ready to rock!

Dance the night away under your very own disco ball. Or add a Lava lamp, Chinese lanterns, or other funky lighting.

Find out-of-the-way but reachable places for equipment like your video camera or karaoke machine.

Cover the food table with a colorful paper tablecloth to brighten up the room—and make cleanup easier!

Toss glitter confetti on the tabletop for a sparkly accent.

Drape a tablecloth over a phone book or a shoe box. Use the raised platform to show off your cake or another centerpiece.

Cool Things to Do with Balloons

Balloon Sky
Tie long ribbons onto the ends of helium-filled balloons. Let the balloons rise to the ceiling so that the ribbons hang down to create a fun "fringe" effect for guests to dance under. For extra fun, tie a little favor or penny candy onto the end of each ribbon.

Balloon Cloud
Cover the floor with so many balloons that you have to gently kick them out of the way to walk through. (Clear them away before dancing, though.)

Balloon Arch
Tape balloons around a doorway to frame the entrance to the party room.

Balloon Bouquet
No helium? Try this quick lift trick. Tie 2 or 3 balloons together with ribbon, then tape the "bouquet" to the end of a dowel. Place the bouquet in a large cup or vase for display.

Balloon Shower
String a net across an upper corner of your party room and fill it with balloons. At the right moment, pull down the net and let the balloons shower your guests.

Balloon Curtain
Cut pieces of string to the length of a doorway. Tie balloons along the strings, placing them about 5 inches apart from each other. Tape or tie the strings to a dowel and hang it above a doorway to create a curtain.

Balloon Animals
Twist long, thin balloons into cute shapes like poodles, flowers, or funky hats.

Seven Steps to Blowing Up a Balloon

1. Stretch and pull the neck of the balloon to loosen it up.

2. Take a deep breath, close lips around the mouth of the balloon, and blow long and steady.

3. When you need more air, clamp the neck of the balloon closed with your fingers and catch your breath.

4. Continue blowing and catching your breath until the balloon is fully inflated.

5. To tie off the balloon, open fingers around the neck slightly and let out a little bit of air. This will make the balloon "softer" and easier to knot.

6. Stretch the neck around two fingers and roll the mouth through the loop, making a knot.

7. Stretch the knot gently to tighten and to make sure air doesn't leak out.

Dizzy from lack of air? Think about buying a balloon pump—available at party or costume stores.

Most-Loved

Girls love easy-to-eat finger foods! Offer a mix of sweet, salty, spicy, and sour treats to satisfy every craving.

Munchies
Chex Mix
Veggies & Ranch Dip
Mini Hot Dogs
in BBQ Sauce
Sub Sandwiches
Sour Gummi Worms
Popcorn

7 Punches

1.

8 cups **7-Up +** 6 scoops **rainbow sherbet =**

Rainbow Punch

2.

8 cups **7-Up +** 3 cups **pineapple juice +** ½ cup **coconut milk =**

Pineapple Coolada

Float pineapple rings on top.

3.

8 cups **7-Up +** 3 cups **cranberry juice cocktail =**

Cranberry Cooler

4.

8 cups **7-Up +** 3 cups **apple juice +** 4 scoops of **vanilla ice cream =**

Apple Pie Smoothie

Sprinkle a dash of cinnamon on top.

5.

8 cups **7-Up +** 3 cups **sparkling white grape juice =**

Snow White

Drop grapes in the bottom of each cup.

with 7-Up*

6.

8 cups **7-Up +** 3 cups **orange juice +** ½ cup **grenadine syrup =**

Plop a cherry into each cup.

Sunrise Sparkler

7.

5 cups **7-Up +** one 6-oz. can **frozen lemonade concentrate**
+ one 6-oz. can **frozen orange juice concentrate**
+ 2 cups **pineapple juice +** 4 scoops **lime sherbet =**

Party Tarty Punch

*You can use any lemon-lime soda pop for these mouthwatering concoctions! For really cool punch, refrigerate liquids before mixing.

Who Needs

Think out of the Duncan Hines box. Replace the cake with . . .

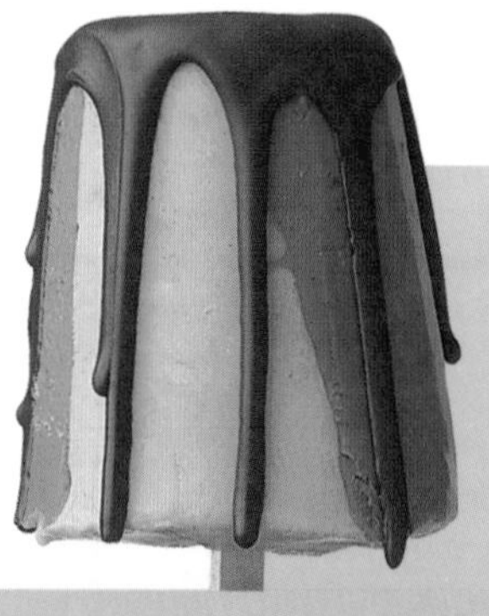

ice cream sundae bars

chocolate fondue

strawberry shortcakes

snow-cones

yogurt smoothies

fruit pizza

giant chocolate-chip cookie

s'mores

fruit Kebabs

marshmallow treats

Cake?

ice cream sandwiches–use waffles, cookies, even pop-tarts®!

Gotta Have Cake?

Quick Cupcakes
Cupcakes are easy to serve and eat. And they're cute, too! If you're short on time, buy plain cupcakes at the store and add your own decorations.

Chocolate or Vanilla?
Satisfy every flavor and frosting combination with a criss-cross cake. Bake one chocolate sheet cake and one vanilla sheet cake. Lay them right next to each other on a tray. Spread vanilla icing on half of the chocolate cake and half of the vanilla cake. Then spread chocolate icing on the remaining halves.

Frills and

Make your party food look as good as it tastes with fun partyware!

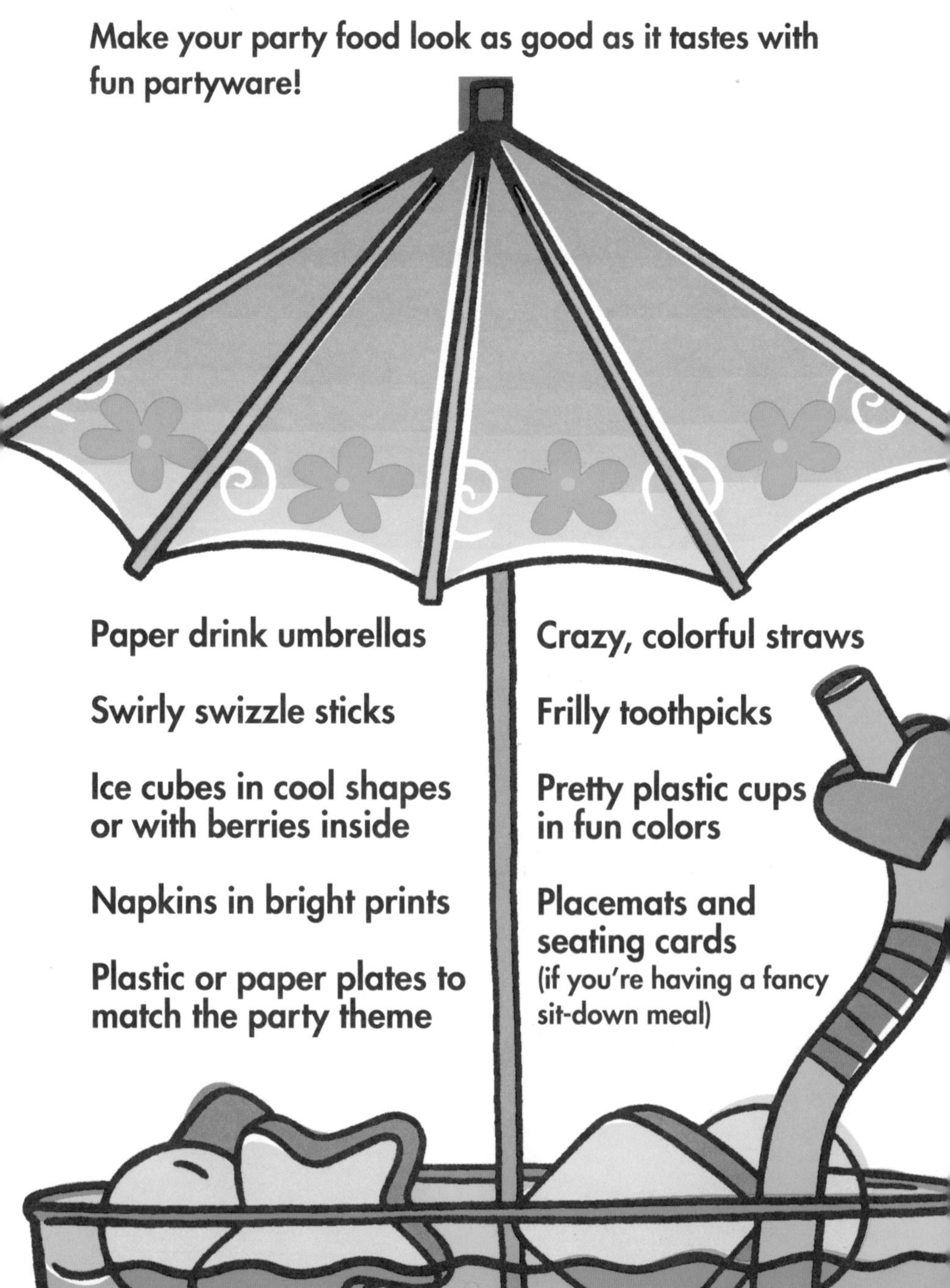

Paper drink umbrellas

Swirly swizzle sticks

Ice cubes in cool shapes or with berries inside

Napkins in bright prints

Plastic or paper plates to match the party theme

Crazy, colorful straws

Frilly toothpicks

Pretty plastic cups in fun colors

Placemats and seating cards (if you're having a fancy sit-down meal)

Thrills

When Do We Eat?

Don't serve all the food at the beginning of the party. Have appetizers and snacks for munching when guests arrive. Then serve the main meal after you've had a chance to play some games, dance, and do other activities you've planned.

Hold Everything

Put food in nice bowls or baskets, or on plates or platters—not in the package it came in. Even potato chips look tastier when they're out of the bag!

Bundle-Ware

Make it easy for munchers to pick up their silverware in one neat bundle. Roll up a fork, knife, and spoon in a party napkin, and tie the bundle closed with ribbon or a party-favor scrunchie.

Free Refills

Try to keep serving dishes full but not overflowing. Every once in a while, refill bowls of pretzels, chips, and dip. Take empty dishes to the kitchen.

Stay Cool

Buy a bag of ice before the party or start making ice cubes in your freezer a day before the party. (Use muffin pans to make giant ice cubes for a punch bowl.) A few minutes before guests arrive, put cubes in an ice bucket or a bowl with tongs or an ice scoop. If you're going outside, load up a cooler.

Today's Specials

Put little signs next to foods to let your guests know what's what. Or write the party menu on a chalkboard and place it nearby. That way, girls can avoid dishing out food they are allergic to or don't like.

Party Smarts

Keep a "to do" list and check off tasks as you do them.

Use one of the Party Planners from the back of the book to track all the things you have to do and to record all your party details in one place. Complete a few tasks every week, and the next thing you know, it'll be party time!

Party Secret #3

Be a Great Hostess.

A great party starts with you—the hostess! You're not only the **girl of the hour** but also the graceful **wizard behind the curtain,** pushing buttons and pulling levers to bring the party to life. So before guests arrive, tuck these entertaining tips under your party hat, and you'll be set to **charm your guests.**

How to Be a Great Hostess

1. **Turn on the charm.** A hostess's number-one job is to make all her guests feel comfortable and welcome. Greet everyone with a smile and tell each guest how glad you are that she could come.

2. During the party, keep your **eyes on the action.** Are people getting tired of the game you're playing? Switch to a new activity. Do your guests look weak from hunger? Bring out the snacks a little earlier. Be flexible!

3. **Laugh it off.** Even if you've planned carefully, something may go wrong. Remember that it's not the end of your party. If you keep your sense of humor, the flub might even make the day more fun.

4. Mingle and move your feet. Go ahead—be the life of the party. Chat away, laugh lots, and be the first one on the dance floor! **Have a good time,** and your friends will, too.

5.
Be yourself. After all, your friends came to your party because they like you.

Fitting Room

Dress yourself in a smart party outfit.

Consider clothes, accessories, or hairstyles that you've gotten a lot of compliments on in the past—they'll make great **conversation starters.**

Pretty clips or a **headband** that go with your outfit and keep hair neat

One or two pieces of **jewelry,** like a beaded bracelet with matching necklace

Fun shirt with details that you love—a colorful print, ruffles, or ribbon trim

Favorite jeans, skirt, or breezy capri pants

Cute, **comfy shoes** that you can move around or dance in easily

Party Fashion Tips

- It's important for you to be ready when the first guest arrives, so **give yourself plenty of time** to get dressed. This is harder than it sounds—time will slip by very quickly when you're getting the room ready and setting out the food.

- Dressing up doesn't mean you have to be uncomfortable. Pick clothes that **look and feel good,** and you'll have way more fun at the party.

- When you're choosing what to wear, **think about the games** and activities you've planned. (If you'll be playing Twister, for example, maybe you should rethink that miniskirt!)

Meet & Greet

Can you get your party off to a smart start? At each fork in the road, choose the path with the answer that sounds like what you'd do. If you reach a dead end, you've made a mistake, so go back and try again!

Maze

Not all of your friends know each other, so you . . .

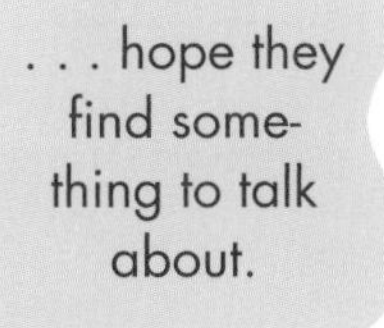

. . . hope they find something to talk about.

. . . introduce each new guest to everyone as she arrives.

It's time to start the party, but two guests haven't arrived yet. You . . .

. . . go ahead with the first game. There's a lot more fun to be had, and you want to make sure you have time for everything you've planned.

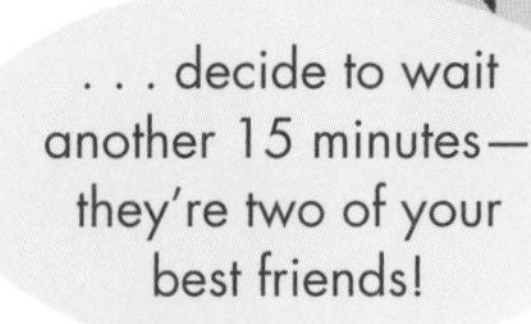

. . . decide to wait another 15 minutes—they're two of your best friends!

Finish!

Breaking

As guests begin to arrive, warm up the room with these conversation starters.

"How did you do your hair like that?"

"Cool shoes! Where did you get them?"

"What do you think of Candy Machine's new CD?"

"Did you see that game? Why didn't the coach call a time-out?"

"Try the pineapple salsa and let me know what you think of it."

"What did you see at Sea World?"

"What do you think of our new science teacher?"

Talking Tips

To get someone in a chatty mood, ask her about herself. For most people, it's a favorite topic!

Avoid questions that can be answered yes or no, like, "So, do you live near the new stadium?" Instead, ask something like, "What's it like inside the stadium since they rebuilt it?"

Keep away from subjects that might make your guest uncomfortable, like grades or making tryouts.

the Ice

May I Introduce . . . ?

If your guests don't know each other, introduce them. When you make an introduction, provide more information than just names. That way, the two people will have something to talk about.

Get-Loose Games

All About You

Pass around a bowl of M&Ms and ask guests to grab a handful but not to eat them yet! Then close your eyes, pick one M&M from the bowl, and call out the color. Each guest counts how many candies she has of the same color and has to tell the others that many things about herself, like fave food or most embarrassing moment.

Zodiac Check

Ask guests their signs and read each person her horoscope from the newspaper.

What If . . .

Ask guests juicy questions like, "What if you were a long-lost member of a royal family?" or "If you were an animal, what kind would you be?"

Secret Star

Tape a picture of a different celebrity on each guest's back (no peeking!). Players ask one another questions about their celebrity to figure out who it is, but they can't ask for the name. If you want to make it harder, allow only questions that can be answered yes or no.

Amaze your guests with ... Party Tricks!

Amazing Grape

Use your thumb to hold a toothpick along the palm side of your index finger. Stick a grape onto the end of the toothpick and hold your finger up so that it looks like you're balancing the grape. Pretend it's hard to balance. Then toss the grape to a friend and challenge her to balance it. Throw away the toothpick when no one is looking!

Singing Soda

Fill a stemmed, crystal wine glass or water goblet with soda. Set the glass on a table, hold the base firmly with one hand, and rub your finger around the rim until the glass starts to sing.

Bubble Magic

Drop a grape into a glass filled with sparkling water or clear soda. When the grape reaches the bottom, rub your finger around the rim of the glass and recite some hocus-pocus words like, "Boil and bubble, toil and trouble." The grape will *magically* rise to the top!

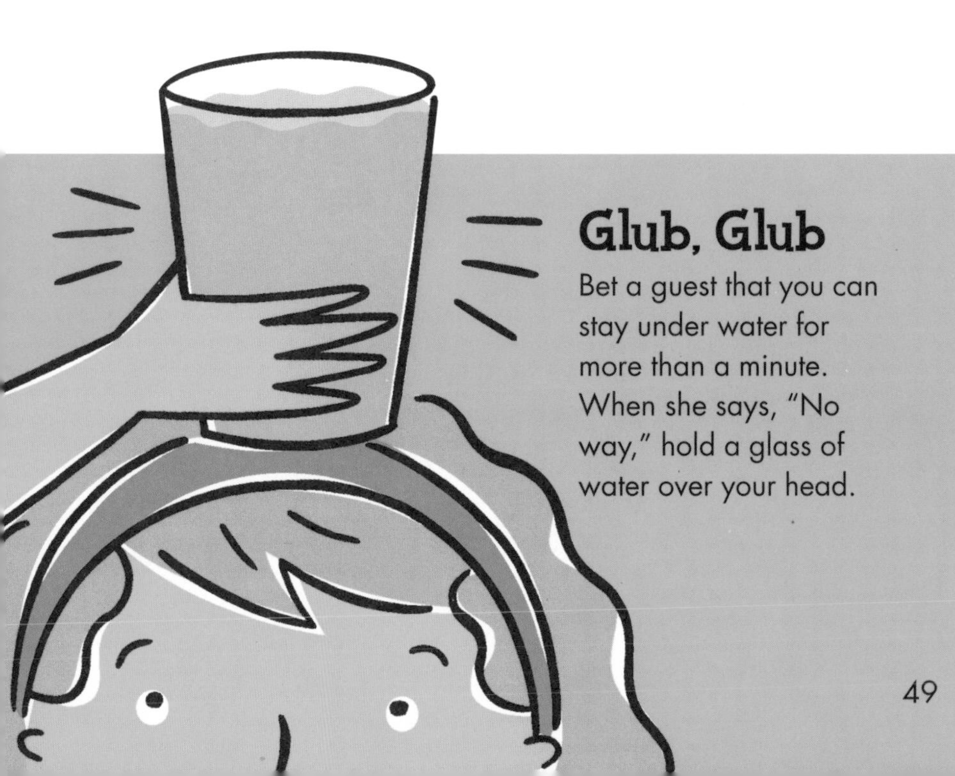

Glub, Glub

Bet a guest that you can stay under water for more than a minute. When she says, "No way," hold a glass of water over your head.

Having Fun Yet?: The Game

Roll a die and see if you can make the right party moves.

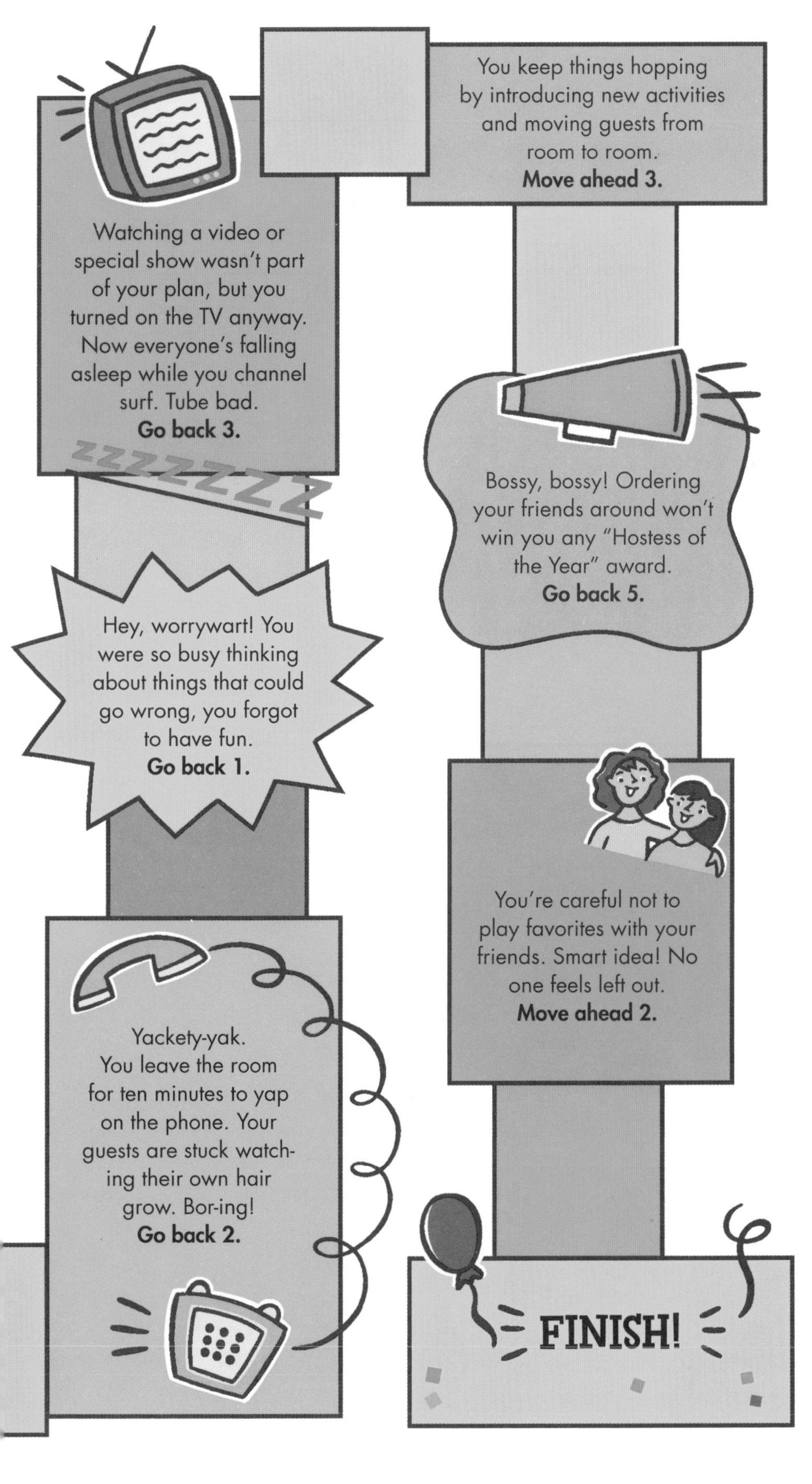

Watching a video or special show wasn't part of your plan, but you turned on the TV anyway. Now everyone's falling asleep while you channel surf. Tube bad. Go back 3.
ZZZZZZZ
Hey, worrywart! You were so busy thinking about things that could go wrong, you forgot to have fun. Go back 1.
Yackety-yak. You leave the room for ten minutes to yap on the phone. Your guests are stuck watching their own hair grow. Bor-ing! Go back 2.
You keep things hopping by introducing new activities and moving guests from room to room. Move ahead 3.
Bossy, bossy! Ordering your friends around won't win you any "Hostess of the Year" award. Go back 5.
You're careful not to play favorites with your friends. Smart idea! No one feels left out. Move ahead 2.
FINISH!

Party Pooper

Here's what to do if you spot a spoilsport in your bunch.

Her motto: "Don't mind me. I'll just sit over here in the corner, sighing."

What to do: Invite her to join every activity, but don't embarrass her by forcing her to do anything. Make sure she's been introduced to everyone, and seat her next to someone who shares an interest of hers, like gymnastics or art. Give her a little time to warm up and get used to the scene.

Her motto: "Look at me! Look at me!"

What to do: When she blurts out the answer to a trivia question for the fourth time, nicely say, "Let's give someone else a chance to play." And if she tries to take over the party, ask her to help refill snack bowls or set up the next game. Putting her to "work" will make her feel important and keep her busy.

Troubleshooter

Her motto: "I don't wanna."

What to do: Say, "The rest of us are going to play. You don't have to join in, but I think you'll be missing out. I've played this game before, and it's really fun."

Her motto: "It's not a party until I break something—a rule, a mirror, whatever!"

What to do: Try to distract her from her wild ways by getting her involved in one of your calmer planned activities. If nothing seems to work, quietly ask an adult to help get her under control.

Party Smarts

There's one more thing for you, the hostess, to do before the guests arrive: **Relax.** That may be easier said than done, but it's important. If you're nervous or stressed out, your guests may pick up on it. Play it cool, and they will, too!

Party Secret #4

Have Fun!

You've planned. You've prepped. You're pepped! Now all that's left to do is **have a blast!** The secret to maximizing the fun is to do stuff that you know your guests love: Play games guaranteed to create **giggles.** Spin music that everyone will want to groove to. And give favors that are sure to bring a **smile.** Your party's going to be just perfect.

Great games

1. Can You Do It?

Hold a relay race using marshmallows stacked on a spoon, or see who can pick up the most M&Ms using chopsticks. You'll have more fun playing silly challenge games like these than you will winning them!

2. Scavenger Hunt

Who doesn't love a little "snoop and sleuth" work? Make a list of objects hidden in the party room or things to find in a magazine, then send your guest detectives on a search-and-find mission.

3. Mind Reading

In these "ESP" games, you let one or more players in on a "secret" and see if the others can catch on. For example, while reading magazines at a sleepover, tell two guests to sip their drinks and say "Yum!" every time you turn the page. The other guests have to watch or listen very closely to uncover the "trigger" and join in.

4. Quiz Biz

Test your guests' trivia knowledge with quizzes and guess-who games. Games like 20 Questions, Name That Movie, or Celebrity Who Am I? will keep girls wondering until they find the answer.

5. Tag

A classic game with a gazillion variations—cartoon tag, freeze tag, flashlight tag. Make up your own game to fit your party theme by changing the safe word, the home base, or the object "It" uses to tag players.

Great Game Tips

Mix quiet games with rowdier ones. Everyone will stay interested—and your party won't get out of control!

Don't forget to **explain the rules**—and make sure everyone understands them.

Divide guests into teams randomly so that friends don't stick together and exclude others. One idea: Put an equal number of red and black checkers in a paper bag. (You should have the same number of checkers as guests.) Have guests pick from the bag to decide which team they'll be on—red or black.

Plan more games than you think you'll need. A game that you thought would take a long time to play might last only a few minutes.

If everyone loves one particular game, **play** it again!

Not-So-Cool Games

Ouch

Games that might hurt someone's feelings are a major party problem. And games like Truth or Dare, which some people enjoy, can make others uncomfortable.

Danger!

Nix games that could lead to someone getting hurt—like Rollerblading through an obstacle course or trampoline challenges. Any activity that involves running with food in a player's mouth is unsafe.

You're Out!

Avoid games that leave some people out of the action with nothing to do, even for a while. The fun stops for anyone who has to sit on the sidelines.

Prizes?

When some people get great prizes and others get nothing, the result is jealousy—and you don't want that at your bash! Try to give prizes to everyone or don't give any at all. For example, if you're tossing leis around a bottle of soda, everyone gets to keep her lei and have a glass of soda when you're all finished. If you do have prizes, make them very small, inexpensive ones that cost the same.

Easy Party

Keep fun at your fingertips with these surefire activities.

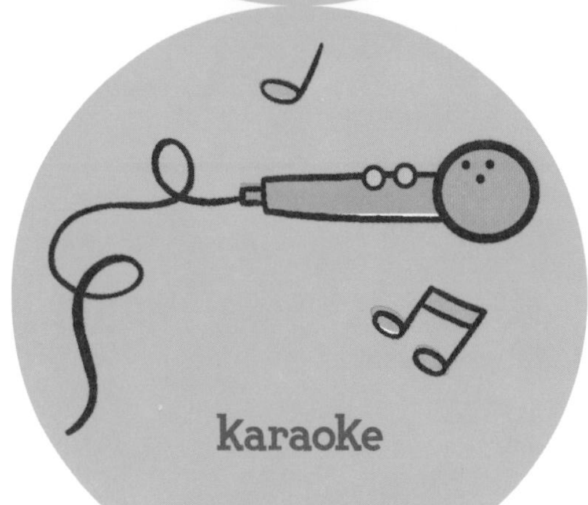

Karaoke

twister®

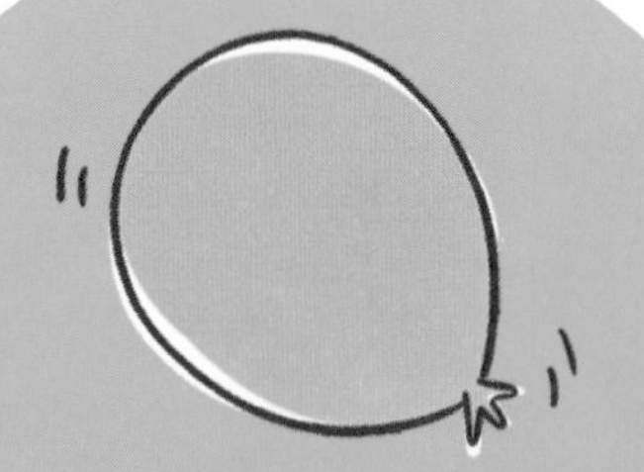

balloon volleyball

magic 8-ball®

fingernail painting

butcher paper for doodling and signing autographs

Pleasers

photo poses

playing cards

hairdo-overs

quizzes

mad-libs®

charades

omen, Anne of Green Gables, The Pokey Little Puppy, Little House on the Prairie, Lord of the Rings, The Princess & the Pea, The Diary of Anne Frank, The Hunchback of Notre Dame, Winnie the Pooh, Curious George, The Cat in the Hat **TV Shows** — The Brady Bunch, Full House, I Love Lucy, Malcolm in the Middle, The Price Is Right, Sa

Charades Mix 'n'

Brush up on your charades skills by matching each signal with its correct meaning.

- ________ **Book**
- ________ **Movie**
- ________ **TV show**
- ________ **Sounds like**
- ________ **Long word**
- ________ **Short word**
- ________ **Getting closer!**
- ________ **Number of words**
- ________ **Drama**
- ________ **Comedy**
- ________ **Not even close!**
- ________ **You're right!**

Cup hand behind your ear.

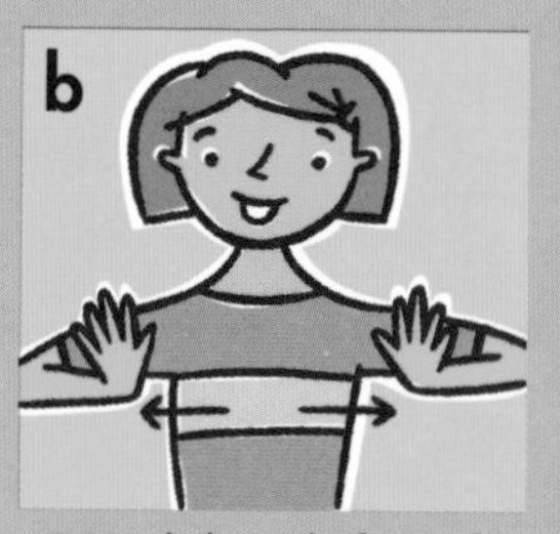

Stretch hands from front of chest out to sides.

Place hands together and unfold.

Pretend you're playing a violin.

Smile widely and slap hand on knee.

Shade eyes and pretend to use a video camera.

Wave hands toward body.

Hold out hand to signal "stop."

Answers: d, h, f, a, b, l, j, i, e, g, k, c.

Match

Touch finger to nose.

Draw a square in the air with your fingers.

Hold up a number of fingers.

Hold two fingers an inch apart.

Prep to Play

Before the party, ask parents or siblings to write the titles of movies, books, or TV shows on slips of paper and put them in a hat. (Otherwise, if you do it, you'll know all the answers.) It's best to use titles containing words that can be acted out easily, like *The Lion King*. Read TV and movie listings for more ideas.

Action!

At the party, divide into two teams. Have a player from one team draw a slip of paper and read it to herself. Then have her act out the title using hand signals and gestures only—she's not allowed to say anything! Her teammates have three minutes to guess the title. When time is up, a player from the next team draws a slip and her teammates try to guess the title. The first team to guess three titles wins!

Put these titles in your hat! Movies— Star Wars, The Wizard of Oz, The Little Mermaid, Popeye, Jaws, Honey I Shrunk the Kids, Doctor Dolittle, Free Willy, Home Alone, Titanic, Planet of the Apes, How the Grinch Stole Christmas, Spy Kids **Books—** Charlotte's Web, Treasure Islar

e Teenage Witch, The Simpsons, Survivor

Can't-Miss Crafts

Make fast and easy party keepsakes with guests.

Instant Rings

Thread beads, buttons, and other baubles onto a twist tie. Wrap around your finger and twist to fit.

Bendy Blooms

Bend and shape pipe cleaners into funky flowers. Put a bee in your bloom by twisting a yellow pipe cleaner around a pencil, gluing on wiggly eyes, and adding little antennae.

'Zine Magnets

Cut pictures or words out of magazines and stick them onto self-adhesive magnetic sheets (available at craft stores). Add glitter or rhinestones for extra sparkle. Trim to fit.

yeehah!

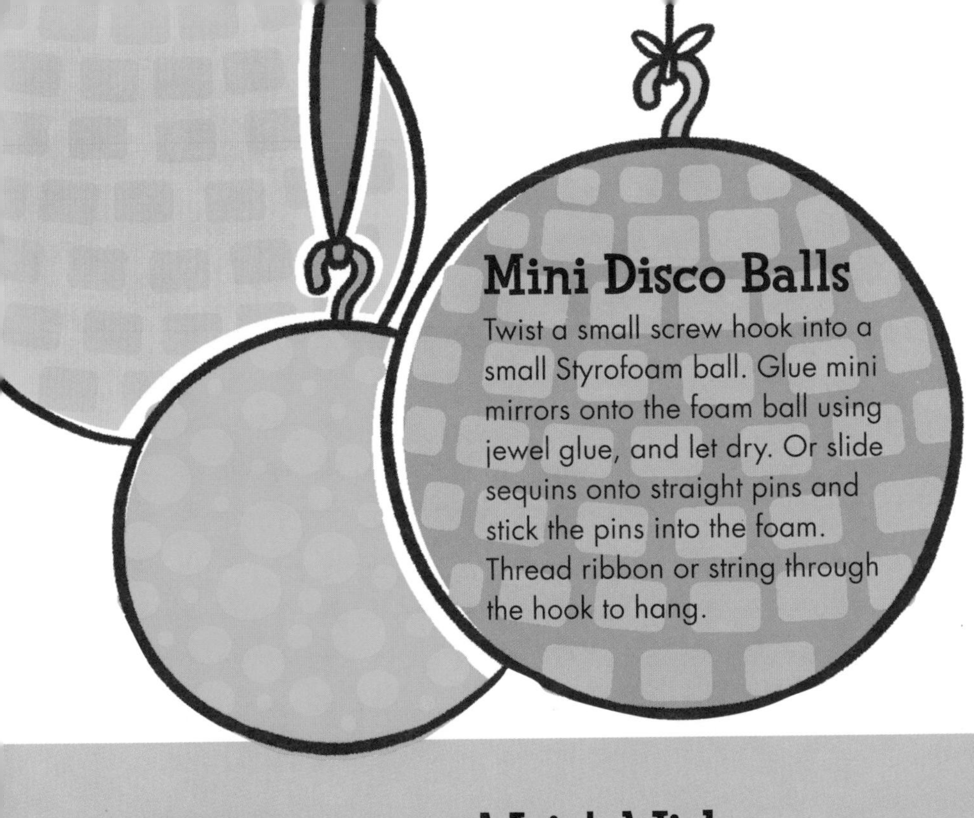

Mini Disco Balls

Twist a small screw hook into a small Styrofoam ball. Glue mini mirrors onto the foam ball using jewel glue, and let dry. Or slide sequins onto straight pins and stick the pins into the foam. Thread ribbon or string through the hook to hang.

Wrist Wish

Use markers or gel pens to write a wish or inspirational word on a thick, brightly colored rubber band. Once ink is dry, wear it on your wrist until your wish comes true!

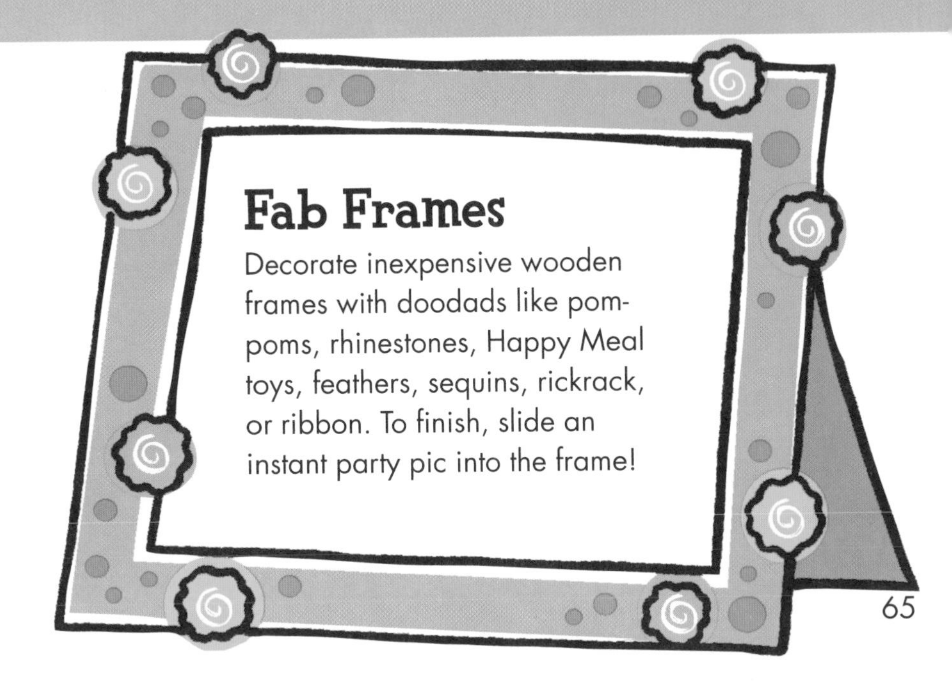

Fab Frames

Decorate inexpensive wooden frames with doodads like pom-poms, rhinestones, Happy Meal toys, feathers, sequins, rickrack, or ribbon. To finish, slide an instant party pic into the frame!

Must-Dance Music

10 songs guaranteed to make guests get a groove on!

YMCA
The Village People

All Star
Smash Mouth

Dancing Queen
ABBA/A-teens

Got to Be Real
Cheryl Lynn

I Love Rock 'n' Roll
Joan Jett/Britney Spears

Music
Madonna

How to Fill a Dance Floor

1. Cue up a song that *everyone* loves.

2. Turn up the volume and turn down the lights to give the room a dance-friendly mood.

3. Make a beeline to the middle of the dance floor and start moving. Wave for others to join you.

4. If a song has specific steps that guests don't know, teach them!

Make Your Own Mix

Burn or record your party tunes onto one CD or tape so that you won't miss out on any fun while fiddling with the stereo. Blend new songs with old favorites. Follow hip-hop with pop, 80s new wave with 70s disco. Surprise guests at the end of the party with a copy of your soundtrack to take home.

Dance Chart

Psst!

There's no right or wrong way to dance. Just relax and move to the music. If you feel good about what you're doing, that will come through in your dancing.

All Together

In the Spotlight

Make a circle on the dance floor and have everyone take turns dancing in the center—the "spotlight."

Soundtracks

Put on your favorite movie soundtracks, like *Shrek, The Princess Diaries*, or *Grease*. Dance like the characters from the movies.

Act It Out

Make up dance steps that go along with the lyrics of a song to tell the story. For example, if a singer croons "call me," pretend you're talking on a phone. The more dramatic, the better.

Video Moves

For cool dance step ideas, take a close look at dancers on music videos. Try out the steps with your guests.

Now

Ooh! Presents!

Opening gifts is one of life's greatest pleasures. But don't let all the pretty bows mess with your party manners.

Whadja Get?

It's best to wait until the end of the party to open your presents. It'll give your guests a chance to rest and digest. While you open your gifts, have Mom or a friend keep a quick list of who gave you what so that you can personalize your thank-you cards.

It's All Good!

Guests are often anxious to see if you like what they brought for you. So try not to make it seem that you like one present better than the others—even if you do. You certainly don't want any guests going away feeling hurt. Thank each guest equally after opening her gift.

Got Enough Stuff?

Instead of presents for you, think about asking guests to bring things that you can donate to a charity like the Humane Society or a homeless shelter.

Final Fun

As your party winds down, give your guests something to do while they wait to be picked up.

- Have a blank **notebook or memory book** ready, and ask each guest to write a few words about the day before she leaves. The next time you have a party, you can read over the notes and have guests write new entries!

- Take **i-Zone pictures** to put in your memory book, or give them to guests as keepsakes.

- Ask your friends to tell you **what they liked most** about the party. If it was a game or a food, you'll know to do it again at your next get-together.

Fab Favors

Brighten up the end of your party with playful trinkets.

cheap, chic rings

charm necklaces

shimmery nail polish

glitter gel

superstar sunglasses

sparkly super balls

silly stickers

hair thingies

pez®

flavored lip gloss

cute coin purses

feather boas

cool Key chains

disposable cameras

flip-flops

flower leis

Take-Away Tips

Hand out favors at the end of the party. That way, your friends won't be distracted from the games, food, and other fun.

Steer clear of squabbles over who got the best gift! Give equal favors to everyone—no special treatment for your best friends.

Let your imagination run wild! For favor inspiration, think about your party theme or the latest fads at school.

Go beyond the bag with these favor-container alternatives:

- cosmetic cases
- mini lunch boxes
- recycled mint tins
- Chinese takeout containers
- mini purses

Party Review

You had a great time! But were there things that you'd do differently for your next party?

Answer these questions now, while your memory is fresh—and use what you learned to make your next party even better!

1. How many guests came to your party? Was it too many people to handle, too few, or just the right number?

2. What was the most fun party moment for you? What did guests seem to enjoy most?

3. What activity could you do without at your next bash?

4. Did your DJ (maybe it was you) keep everyone in the party mood? What music were you missing that you'd like to play at your next shindig?

5. Which foods did guests scarf down the second you brought them out? Which ones were less popular?

6. What took the most time to prepare? What could you do differently to cut down on the amount of work (for example, getting an ice cream cake instead of baking one yourself)?

7. Did any problems come up? What can you do to avoid the problems at your next party?

8. One last question: Did you learn any party secrets of your own? What do you think is the key to a great party?

Party Smarts

What's the most important thing to do after a party? Clean up!

Your parents will be more likely to let you have another party if they see that you've been responsible for this one from beginning to end. Break out the trash bags and start with the big stuff.

Party Secret #5

Be a Great Guest.

An **expert party girl** is more than a fabulous hostess. She's also a terrific guest when it's time to head off to someone else's party! **Be yourself, talk to lots of people, and have fun . . .** sound familiar? But there are more secrets to being a great guest. Read on for the inside scoop!

How to Be a

Remember that it's only a game. Win or lose, be a good sport during party activities. Nothing kills fun faster than a player who whines "Unfair!" or rubs her victory in everyone's face.

Mind your munchie manners. No double-dipping in the salsa. Don't talk with your mouth full. Throw your empty plate and cup away. If you like something, say so. If you don't, don't say so.

Go with the flow. Maybe you think it would be better to play volleyball before you eat the birthday cake. But a good guest doesn't tell the hostess how to run things. For smooth sailing, smile and follow the party plan.

Make yourself useful. Memorize these three words: "Can I help?" Use them often, and your hostess will wonder what she would have done without you!

Great Guest

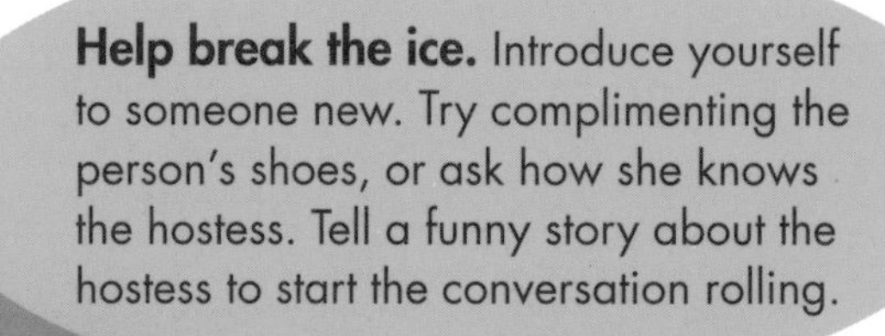

Help break the ice. Introduce yourself to someone new. Try complimenting the person's shoes, or ask how she knows the hostess. Tell a funny story about the hostess to start the conversation rolling.

Be appreciative. Throwing a party is hard work! Show your hostess it was worth it by thanking her at the end of the bash. Then give her a compliment, like, "The decorations were amazing!"

Don't steal the show. This is your hostess's special day. If you insist on being the center of attention, she won't enjoy herself much—and you'll look rude. Instead, propose a toast to her and make her feel great!

Give a thoughtful gift. When going to a birthday party, think about the person you're shopping for. What does she like? What are her favorites? Pick out a present that fits her to a T.

Party Smarts

Don't do anything you wouldn't do at home.

When you go to a friend's bash, act the way you'd want someone to behave at your own party. Follow through and you'll be invited to many more parties!

Party Survival Guide

The cat walked through the cake! Everyone hated a game! You spilled punch on the carpet! Mishaps happen, but don't despair. Whether you're a guest or the hostess, there's a way to save just about any sticky situation.

Problem?

You look around the crowd . . . and don't recognize a single face except the hostess's!

Solution!

Look for someone who's not too deep in conversation, and introduce yourself. Take a look at the icebreakers and advice on page 46 for help on what to say. Be friendly and not too pushy. If the conversation doesn't take off, move on and introduce yourself to someone else.

Problem?

Crash! You break or spill something.

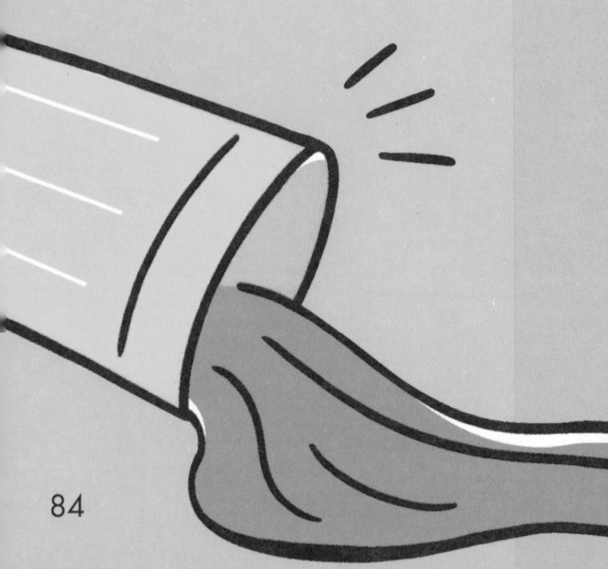

Solution!

Though you may feel terrible, don't lose your cool. Apologize sincerely, and help clean up the best you can. Everyone knows accidents happen, and a good hostess will forgive you. If you're the hostess and a guest breaks something, treat the accident like a minor glitch. Clean up quickly, and move on to the next item on your party agenda!

Problem?

You say the wrong thing, and it feels like all eyes are on you.

Solution!

If you hurt someone's feelings with your slip of the lip, apologize immediately. If you said something embarrassing or silly, try to make a joke of it and laugh it off. Then change the subject quickly. Chances are, everyone else will forget your mistake much sooner than you will!

Problem?

Yawn. This party is *sooo* boring!

Solution!

If it's your party, ask guests what games they'd like to play or what music they'd like to hear. If you're a guest and the hostess seems to be out of ideas, politely suggest an activity you think would be fun: "Hey, does anyone like to play charades?" Look on pages 60 and 61 for some sure-fire ideas.

Problem?

It's a sleepover, and you're homesick.

Solution!

If you know that you get homesick at sleepovers, plan ahead by bringing your own pillow so that you have something familiar. And don't be shy about calling home! Sometimes a few words from your mom or dad are all it takes. If nothing works, ask to be picked up right before everyone goes to sleep. That way, you'll still get to enjoy most of the party, but you'll sleep in your own bed.

Problem?

Uh-oh. Everyone's dancing, but you have two left feet!

Solution!

You'll stand out more if you make a point of refusing to dance. So get out on the floor and try your best. Don't try anything too wild—just move to the beat or imitate what everyone else is doing. Maybe you'll finally learn how to dance! Check pages 68 and 69 for dancing tips. If you still don't feel comfortable, keep yourself busy with some other activity—take charge of the music or take photos.

Problem?

Mean gossip is making you uncomfortable.

Solution!

Gossiping about people who aren't at the party may seem natural to some. But mean words often come back to haunt you when feelings get hurt, and it can poison the atmosphere of a party. If you're the hostess, start a new activity or game to keep everyone's mind off the gossip. If you're a guest, try to change the topic, or walk away and talk with another group of guests.

Problem?

Someone dares you to play a mean prank on another guest.

Solution!

You know that pranks are wrong. So how do you resist when everyone else is in on it? Say, "I'd rather do something that we can *all* have fun with." If others call you chicken, try a funny reply. Smile and joke, "Yeah, see my wings?" Chances are, they'll let you off the hook. If it's your party, you can also quietly ask your parents to stop the pranks.

Problem?

You're not sure what that is on the food table!

Solution!

Weird or unfamiliar food may not be as strange as you think. Ask the hostess what's in it. Try it if you think you might like it. But if you don't, don't make a face or shriek, "Yuck!" Just pass by the suspect dish and eat something else.

Problem?

The party's over . . . but one of your guests seems to be camping out by the cheese dip.

Solution!

You're stuck with a guest who won't leave—but don't let that turn into an awkward situation. Instead, go ahead and start cleaning up, and nicely ask your friend to help out. You can have fun working together and talking about the party. Or maybe she'll just take the hint and head home.

Party Planner

Don't throw a party without it!

Guest List

	R.S.V.P.?		R.S.V.P.?
	☐		☐
	☐		☐
	☐		☐
	☐		☐
	☐		☐

Date to send invitations:

Party Details

Date & Time:

Theme:

Colors:

Decorations:

Party Favors:

Special Equipment Needed

- ☐ CD player
- ☐ mood lighting/party lights
- ☐ camera with film
- ☐ camcorder (charge battery)
- ☐ karaoke machine
- ☐ other

Music

Yum!

Main Meal:

Munchies:

Cake & Sweets:

Drinks:

Games

Game 1:

Game 2:

Game 3:

Game 4:

More things to do:

Party Countdown

4 Weeks Ahead

- ❑ Decide on date, time, theme, and location of your party. Make reservations at a location if necessary.
- ❑ Send out invitations. Keep a guest list so you can keep track of people who R.S.V.P.
- ❑ Start planning decorations, food, and favors.

3 Weeks Ahead

- ❑ Start buying paper plates, napkins, decorations, and other party stuff.
- ❑ Plan activities or games.
- ❑ Talk to your family about how they can help.

1 Week Ahead

- ❑ Decide what food you'll serve and start a party shopping list.
- ❑ Gather things you'll need for activities or games.
- ❑ Check your guest list and count how many people have R.S.V.P.'d. (You may want to check with anyone who hasn't responded.)
- ❑ If the party is at another location, confirm your reservation.

2 Days Ahead

- ❑ Decide what to wear to the party and make sure it's clean.
- ❑ Do a final check on what you have. Add what you still need to your shopping list and buy it.
- ❑ Pick out music CDs to play.
- ❑ Write up a party plan to keep the fun on track.

1 Day Ahead

- ❑ Make food that will keep for a day, such as cookies or a cake.

Party Day

- ❑ Set up the party room: rearrange furniture, put up lights, decorate!
- ❑ Prepare the food or place a take-out/delivery order for things like pizza, if necessary.
- ❑ Get dressed.
- ❑ Set out snacks and drinks.
- ❑ Turn on some music to set the mood.

Party Time!

- ❑ **Have fun.**

Party Planner

Don't throw a party without it!

Guest List

	R.S.V.P.?		R.S.V.P.?
	☐		☐
	☐		☐
	☐		☐
	☐		☐
	☐		☐

Date to send invitations:

Party Details

Date & Time:

Theme:

Colors:

Decorations:

Party Favors:

Special Equipment Needed

- ☐ CD player
- ☐ mood lighting/party lights
- ☐ camera with film
- ☐ camcorder (charge battery)
- ☐ karaoke machine
- ☐ other

Music

Yum!

Main Meal:

Munchies:

Cake & Sweets:

Drinks:

Games

Game 1:

Game 2:

Game 3:

Game 4:

More things to do:

Party Countdown

4 Weeks Ahead

- ❐ Decide on date, time, theme, and location of your party. Make reservations at a location if necessary.
- ❐ Send out invitations. Keep a guest list so you can keep track of people who R.S.V.P.
- ❐ Start planning decorations, food, and favors.

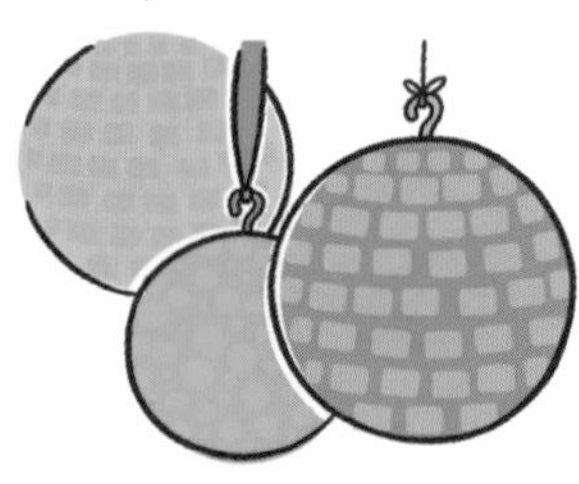

3 Weeks Ahead

- ❐ Start buying paper plates, napkins, decorations, and other party stuff.
- ❐ Plan activities or games.
- ❐ Talk to your family about how they can help.

1 Week Ahead

- ❐ Decide what food you'll serve and start a party shopping list.
- ❐ Gather things you'll need for activities or games.
- ❐ Check your guest list and count how many people have R.S.V.P.'d. (You may want to check with anyone who hasn't responded.)
- ❐ If the party is at another location, confirm your reservation.

2 Days Ahead

- ❐ Decide what to wear to the party and make sure it's clean.
- ❐ Do a final check on what you have. Add what you still need to your shopping list and buy it.
- ❐ Pick out music CDs to play.
- ❐ Write up a party plan to keep the fun on track.

1 Day Ahead

- ❐ Make food that will keep for a day, such as cookies or a cake.

Party Day

- ❐ Set up the party room: rearrange furniture, put up lights, decorate!
- ❐ Prepare the food or place a take-out/delivery order for things like pizza, if necessary.
- ❐ Get dressed.
- ❐ Set out snacks and drinks.
- ❐ Turn on some music to set the mood.

Party Time!

- ❐ **Have fun.**

Party Planner

Don't throw a party without it!

Guest List

	R.S.V.P.?		R.S.V.P.?
	❐		❐
	❐		❐
	❐		❐
	❐		❐
	❐		❐

Date to send invitations:

Party Details

Date & Time:

Theme:

Colors:

Decorations:

Party Favors:

Special Equipment Needed

- ❐ CD player
- ❐ mood lighting/party lights
- ❐ camera with film
- ❐ camcorder (charge battery)
- ❐ karaoke machine
- ❐ other

Music

Yum!

Main Meal:

Munchies:

Cake & Sweets:

Drinks:

Games

Game 1:

Game 2:

Game 3:

Game 4:

More things to do:

Party Countdown

4 Weeks Ahead

- ❐ Decide on date, time, theme, and location of your party. Make reservations at a location if necessary.
- ❐ Send out invitations. Keep a guest list so you can keep track of people who R.S.V.P.
- ❐ Start planning decorations, food, and favors.

3 Weeks Ahead

- ❐ Start buying paper plates, napkins, decorations, and other party stuff.
- ❐ Plan activities or games.
- ❐ Talk to your family about how they can help.

1 Week Ahead

- ❐ Decide what food you'll serve and start a party shopping list.
- ❐ Gather things you'll need for activities or games.
- ❐ Check your guest list and count how many people have R.S.V.P.'d. (You may want to check with anyone who hasn't responded.)
- ❐ If the party is at another location, confirm your reservation.

2 Days Ahead

- ❐ Decide what to wear to the party and make sure it's clean.
- ❐ Do a final check on what you have. Add what you still need to your shopping list and buy it.
- ❐ Pick out music CDs to play.
- ❐ Write up a party plan to keep the fun on track.

1 Day Ahead

- ❐ Make food that will keep for a day, such as cookies or a cake.

Party Day

- ❐ Set up the party room: rearrange furniture, put up lights, decorate!
- ❐ Prepare the food or place a take-out/delivery order for things like pizza, if necessary.
- ❐ Get dressed.
- ❐ Set out snacks and drinks.
- ❐ Turn on some music to set the mood.

Party Time!

- ❐ **Have fun.**

no

yes

make it your wish on your next birthday

nah

only time will tell

no

sure thing

out to lunch–try again in 5 minutes

yes

maybe

maybe

yes

dream on . . .

without a doubt!

no

don't hold your breath

oui, oui

keep your fingers crossed

yes

no

Instant Party Fun!

Just add dice.

Magic Q&A Game

All your questions answered!

You will need:

a die

lots of questions

How to Play:

1. Tear this page out of the book.

2. Place on a surface answer-side up.

3. Take turns asking yes-or-no questions out loud and rolling the die—with eyes closed! The answers lie where the die lands.

Could there be a better party than this one?

Will I ever get a horse?

Does Max like Marcy?

Will Lucie become a rock star?

Will I find the key to my diary?